THE WATER STEALER

MAURICE RIORDAN

The Water Stealer

faber and faber

First published in 2013
by Faber and Faber Ltd
Bloomsbury House
74–77 Great Russell Street
London WC1B 3DA

Typeset by RefineCatch Ltd, Bungay, Suffolk
Printed in England by T. J. International Ltd, Padstow, Cornwall

A CIP record for this book
is available from the British Library

ISBN 978-0-571-30245-1

FSC
www.fsc.org
MIX
Paper from
responsible sources
FSC® C101712

2 4 6 8 10 9 7 5 3 1

in memory of Gregory, Mike, Michael

and for Kathryn

Acknowledgements

Thanks are due to the following publications, where some of these poems appeared: *Agenda, Irish Times, Manchester Review, Magma, Matter, Modern Poetry in Translation, New Statesman, The Penguin Book of Irish Poetry* (edited by Patrick Crotty), *Poetry International, Poetry Ireland, Poetry London, Poetry Review, Riddlefence, The Spectator, this corner, The Wake Forest Series of Irish Poetry* (edited by Conor O'Callaghan), *The Word Hoard* (edited by Greg Delanty and Michael Matto).

'The Cranium' was commissioned by The Poetry Society for the exhibition 'Leonardo da Vinci: Anatomist' at The Queen's Gallery.

I am grateful to the Centre Culturel Irlandais for a residency in 2011 which enabled me to work on this collection.

My thanks, too, to Kathryn Maris and Matthew Hollis.

Contents

THE WATER STEALER

the eye crosses a flooded river
– Zulu proverb

The Lull

It happened on the cinder path between the playing field
and the graveyard one afternoon in October
when all the leaves of the aspen flipped over
and stayed, the way a skirt might blow up and hold
in a gust of wind – except there was no wind,
one of those days when the thud of a football
hangs in the deadened air. But there was no thud,
no sound from man or bird. So I'd swear if I'd looked
at my watch just then the digits would have stuck

if I could have looked, for it must've been a time
when time was snagged in its fluid escapement
and in that lull no one can enter the world,
or leave it; the cars stand on the motorway,
the greyhound's legs are knotted above the track,
a missile is framed in mid-flight, no sound
comes from the child's mouth, the open beak,
and the shoal of herring is a sculpted cloud
shimmering under the glass of the rolling downs.

At this moment, when the joker palms the room-key,
the punching fist can be opened, the egg slipped back
under the nesting bird, and each of us could scurry
to forestall one mischance, or undo one wrong choice
whose thorn of consequence has lodged till now,
before whatever it is keeps the world scary
and true breaks loose. A squirrel turns tail
overhead, a chestnut rolls to the ground, and with it
a drawn-out scream arrives from childhood.

The Hare

The boy has come across fields to the ring-fort
– under the barbed wire, through the wet barley,
over the stream. He's listened to the stonechat
on the thorn above Keefe's Well and fingered
the grass where a rabbit slipped out of sight.

Now he approaches the mound in earshot
of the river below – if only he could stop,
he could balance the slender jug of his body
unspilled, while his thought turns on some dream
of football or riding bareback across prairie,

before he's waded into the shoulder-high wave
of bracken onto the fort, and there in the dip
(where Ahern or Carney the Knacker set the trap)
the hare sits on her haunches, her nostrils
twitching between fronds and thistles, so calm

it seems he will gentle her in from the wild,
when his shadow dulls the chestnut of an eye
and she jumps, outstretched in air and free
for a second, but held in the frame of her leap
by the rusted teeth sunk into her hind leg.

So the boy finds a stone, as he must, smooth
as carbolic soap, and aims to connect
with the head – the hare though is quick, as she yanks
and tosses the leg-iron, to herself unwounded.
But she can't snap the raw bone from its grip.

So now he's dense and accurate, until the eyes
go dim, a thread of blood loops from the mouth,
and the hare lies before the boy, who will dream
of the mooncalf that leaned then from the bracken,
and smirking took the stone out of his hand.

Turkeys

appear from the orchard.
There now says Uncle Ned,
pouring us lemonade.
It'll be another scorcher.

The bronze birds drop wing,
shake caruncle and snood
engorged with purple blood,
and rattle in full barding.

My prize cock's gone lame!
He lifts each ringed foot
singly, slowly – to shoot
the short film frame by frame.

On rue Ortolan I hear
the chorus of gobbles
roll across the mossed cobbles
from distant Ophir.

The Dun Cow

What's the Dun Cow doing on the Old Kent Road,
I'm wondering, when who should blow in
But this bucko wearing the moss-green gabardine
My mother wore when out feeding the hens.

Those beaks were taking it in turns to coax
Crushed oats from between her toes, her horny
Old toes covered over with sores, with the bunions
And warts that stuck out through her brogues.

So how're they keeping? There's rheum in his eye.
I had truck with them all – all the old crowd.
Yer da and yer ma, and the man in Dungourney?

Tucked up with their rosaries, they are,
Piled one on the other at home in Lisgoold,
Pushing up daisies many the long year.

The Poacher

At the streak of dawn, in a hunter's mist,
our father vaults the five-bar gate,
and from the hide of the burning whin
he shoots the duck – the drake, that is.
Tonight he'll grace our father's plate.
No harm done, since with the spring
the hen returns to the boggy ground
to breed there with a different drake.
I saw last time as I toured around
(the new shed; where the puncheons stood;
the nettle-mound of the badger sett)
the duck was back with her skittering brood
on the rush-grown pond, the one-time lake.
A different duck, I correct myself.

The Barn

Where no one's been for days, months maybe.

Nothing but mice under the scatter of hay,
swallows and wind in-and-out of the slates.

As I step into the dun light, an owl slips
dream-quick from the corner of my eye.

I must have usurped some horny old Lar,
or fretful ghost at ease here for the night.

The Cross

Vinnie Twomey's miniature of The Cross
perches on the dud TV in Twomey's bar.
It's the view as you come onto the bridge
from Leestown: the Esso pumps out front,
with the store and two pubs over the road,
the sheep-wash glued into the right-hand corner.
And on the slope of the Carrigeen to the rear
stands the Lambert sisters' tiny Swiss chalet
– a model of a model, with corrugated walls
of biscuit tin and a red matchstick verandah.
Everything is made and exact, no attempt
at plants or people, though you'd guess from the sole
of a boot flashing its pin-sized hobnails
that Vinnie's da has just gone through the door
to the snug. And there sure enough he is,
already locked in debate with your own old man.
May Stretch's Mercedes is ticking over outside
at the pumps. You can read its expired tax disc
and dangling number plate, EZB 4,
the nozzle of Extra docked in the tank and taking
so long to fill you wonder has the clock
stopped since you've foolishly wished it to.
The passenger door is open to rain and wind
but you can just hear the tinny radio playing,
and on the air a hornpipe, or a hurling match
being broadcast live from Thurles or Birr.

The Flight

For a good half hour this morning, from five
till the mobile's ringtone woke me in a sweat,
I was young again and Mammy was alive.
I was childless, bookless, clueless, setting out
alone, circuitously on my way to Shannon
with assignations and delays – and no passport,
I realized. I phoned home frantic with a plan.
Would Matty bike it to me at the airport?
But I couldn't keep our mother on the line.
How come you cannot use a phone! I roared.
Then two nieces showed up, grown up, all smiles
in a red MG. I'd no notion who they were.
Yet they took me in. With luck I'd make my flight,
if Mammy now would ring me on my mobile.

The Age of Steam

Last night in the box where you name the person
to inform in the event of death I wrote 'Mother' –
my mother who lives on most nights in my dreams
where I'm young again, alone, home for holidays
or about to fly to Canada – running this time
for the plane (the airport's in the farm next to ours)
while carrying a shorn Christmas tree and worried
will I be allowed to board, when I wake . . . then drift
to a house I've lived in years it seems, spacious,
but with a leaking roof and timber walls so frail
the rickety bedroom's on the point of caving in.
It isn't Surrey Road, and then it is but has
an added room, which somehow all that decade
– the children growing up – I never knew was there,
an old-style parlour with sideboard, knick-knacks,
gramophone, cuckoo clock, and a Sacred Heart
offering its coal of glowing flesh, which coils and swells,
yet is solid in the Virgin's hands, its geometry
elusive, or rather as I wake in the full coherence
of the dream, at the first thought the image slips
beyond perception – as once in Victoria Station
heading for home, for Lisgoold, and about to find
the train to take me there, I stood in bliss under
the departure boards, those mechanical wooden ones,
when with the noise of skittles they flipped to Sanskrit.
But now I'm back in Hickey's passage (the next-door farm)
in a damp, strip-lit tunnel from which I climb into
the yard, a stop on the old Cork-to-Youghal line,
where it's the Age of Steam with limestone walls,
an Avery scales, wrought-iron gates and grilles.

The sky is vast with pinnacled slowly tumbling
cloud palaces, marble-white and interspaced by
lapis blue – an active spring day of wind with the view
across the Weald, the orchards dense with butterflies,
finches, cuckoos – and I am loath to turn for home,
our dark boreen, the leafless privet, vacant dwelling,
when I see it's light outside the curtain, a dawn
of dampened sun, pigeons, trucks on Linden Grove,
the trickle of the water feature, and in my chest
the hissing thumping piston – 14 years on – of grief.

The Larkin Hour

Waking at four to soundless dark, I stare

I woke to a backpacker's vista of empties
and the sight of my plump soft torso gaunt
in streetlight, in a city whose patois escaped
my competence, whose skittish moods and laws
of tense were too crafty-quick, its misshaped
coven of vowels devised, it seems, to taunt
my ear when the throng of youthful voices
hummed at night, barring with ribbons of gauze

entry to stairs and corridors, to concealed
warrens of art and commerce, oak-recessed
alcoves where sly tongues had spent centuries
whispering intrigue and where reposed,
among the old exquisite cruelties,
love's calm and ample tapestry – an almost
touchable proof of appetites fulfilled,
whose code to me nobody had disclosed.

And dragged up out of some weird space
(in which was lodged a sting of infant fear)
I saw I'd held too long the shallow belief
all would be well, that friends and family
would knit a web equal to age and grief
– and to this brought effort, sweat, my cloth ear,
the willingness to put on a brave face,
what I saw was a sham proficiency.

Outside the new day had begun to flood
the roofline, angled to deflect and shatter
in bits the raw light which, as it descends
sheer guttering and sifts down stone mazes,
turns soft, complex, gold to its citizens.
In an hour I, too, would swap my dazzled lair
for the bustling kiosk, and there make good
the damp notes and bandy textbook phrases.

The Cuckoo Clock

for Michael Donaghy, 1954–2004

Parking near St Pancras long before light,
it wouldn't spook if you peered from a shop front
or popped from a grille – remembering the night
we arranged a rendezvous at the Elephant,
you like a meerkat in-and-out of the subways
on the traffic island, head cocked but hesitant
when I called *A Mhíchíl* through the sodium haze
– who already must have felt in your brain a faint
alert above the chug of the Riesenrad . . .
I observed the scared look but never imagined
you'd be panicked or with a farcical skip
be gone: feral, too soft you were, but glad
in your heart as you eyed up the sky, quickened
your step of a sudden, and gave me the slip.

The Navigator

for Michael Murphy, 1965–2009

Always the same seat, gliding backwards, north,
when the dawn broke my side of the Pennines
beyond Newark, where I looked out for herons
on the reddened lake and thought of you in Aigburth
patient in the sky-lit room, this same light
thundering at you like Handel's Philistines
even as the thought struck – how in seconds
it would flood your longed-for West and ignite
the ocean from Benwee to Erris Head . . .
Let me repeat a local's words, wind-caught
as the seas heaved and stretched to Reykjavík:
Wasn't he very brave, Brendan! She shouted,
*Brendan the Navigator – to go out on that
without map or guide in his scrap of currach.*

The Hip-Flask

for Gregory O'Donoghue, 1951–2005

When, twenty-eight years ago, the bus climbs uphill
(and we climbed forever out of Harrisburg, Penn)
you offer me the hip-flask wrapped in its indigo
sleeve, and cite the Tailor: *The world's only a blue
bag, Moss, knock a squeeze out of it while you can!*
I taste the sweet rye a May morning, as we head

for Boston and Robbie's, no inkling of what's ahead
that summer when we'll miss His Nibs of Beacon Hill
but check out the Aquarium – through the glass vents scan
the giant-finned sharks touring their high-rise pen.
It brought to mind your guppy-tank on Brock by blue
Ontario's shore where, in truth, all was about to go

up in flames, the marriage of young minds undergo
alteration as impediments came to a head
and love struck again – as love will – out of the blue;
when with new squeeze, white Goddess, the raven Gail,
you take wing for Grantham to frolic in the open
sesame, hey-ho, of Maggie's England – in which can

of worms surely you were doomed like the last Mohican.
You never made it up the Cydnus. It was no go
the *TLS*, no way Queen Square – not putting a pen
to paper for years since, it seems, you'd plunged head
first into a tide of doubt and were careering downhill
at knots, when the wind turned, an uncanny breeze blew

you home to Cork, where skies cleared Klein-blue
improbably, briefly: two neat books in the can
with one more, your late sweet excellence, on the go
the night you show up – bone-dry, frail – in Carrigtwohill
to launch my *Floods*, brandishing it above your head
as outside on cue the millennial heavens open.

We were back in the banter-ship of ye olde Wig & Pen
disputing into the dawn the ifs and buts of poems till blue
in the face. The heartache of it all goes to my head.
I'm on the Ouse the day – straight-backed as Chief Iffucan –
you claim we're rowing downstream. No question! All go
till we face the weir: *D'ye think, Moss, the water flows uphill?*

If only, Gréagóir. Then this daftness end, cancel the day.
We'll ferry you upstream to the hills of Pennsylvania.
And the blue flask replenish for our long years ahead.

King Alfred's Epilogue to the Pastoral Care
of Gregory the Great

for Greg Delanty

Here is the water which the Lord of all
Pledged for the well-being of his people.
He said it was his wish that water
Should flow forever into this world
Out of the minds of generous men,
Those who serve him under the sky.
But none should doubt the water's source
In Heaven, the home of the Holy Ghost.
It is drawn from there by a chosen few
Who make sacred books their study.
They seek out the tidings they contain,
Then spread the word among mankind.
But some withhold it in their hearts.
They never let it pass their lips
Lest it go to waste in the world.
By this means it stays pure and clear,
A pool within each man's breast.
Others let it flow freely over all the land,
Though care must be taken lest it run
Too loud and fast across the fields,
Transforming them to bogs and fens.
Gather round now with your drinking cups,
Gregory has brought the water to your door.
Fill up, and return again for refills.
If you have come with cups that leak
You must hurry to repair and patch them,
Or else you'll squander the rarest gift,
And the drink of life will be lost to you.

from Old English

Irish

That gleam the sand has before the tide,
its fish-skin-wet and soft-cement texture,
so it stands out as if above the strand
– is there a word for it in Irish? So one
oarsman seeing its oily sheen shouts
Tarraingimís chuige! And the other nods.

In English, there's a word I've forgotten
for those reflections on the underside
of the prow . . . I see them, or their cognates,
when the early sun is on the pond
at home, and it sends bubbles of light
along the dusty mahogany sideboard.

No one I've ever asked knows the word.
And watching the bubbles now like cells
in a Petri dish, it's hard to think one pulse
of code sent brain to brain would bring to mind
their wisp-fire on the creosoted wood,
together with wind and sky this end of day,

the last before we pack our bags and up sticks
for London . . . already there's the *petite mort*
of items missed or chucked, as the boat heads
for port, the rowers pulling crosswind hard
into the swell, and I feel the earth's slow spin
and seasonal lurch in the slight ocean chill.

Yet the word is there in Melville, or Conrad,
where I might still read it; snagged, too, up
some old boreen of memory on a dozen
rusty neurons, from where it could slip loose,
or I'll overhear it spoken on the pier,
or happen on the right philologist.

And then, as the tongue recoups the sound
effortlessly, the word will shed its lure
and be an all-too-easy hook for this effect
of light hitting the sliding planes of water
(which for me also involves my armchair,
the screen, solitude, the grip of coffee).

I'll find there was a gain to the small disablement,
and long for dreams in which I've spoken Irish,
or once Norwegian – no words as such . . .
just a moist pleasurable chemical blaze
of utterance, not unlike that queer looming
of the strand, where the tide has yet to reach.

The New Poetry

after Eochaidh Ó hEoghusa, 1603

Praise be! A turn for the better,
A sudden shift in the weather.
If I don't tap into this new racket
I could end up out of pocket.

Good riddance, then, to the old measures,
To those fussy rules and strictures.
This method's cushier, more enlightened,
And might usher me into the limelight.

Those erstwhile ornamented poems
Fell on deaf ears only – lofty odes
Sailing over the heads of the people,
Like caviar hurled at the general.

If verse of mine from now to the last trump.
Perplex the brain of one Ulster dunce
I'll give back – it's a hefty wager –
Every last farthing of my retainer.

Free verse and the open road!
It's what pots the money ball.
I'll soon be paying off my loans
Courtesy of the Earl Tyrconnell.

No one's going to best yours truly
When it comes to pap and vacuity.
I'll be out there on the fairground
In all weathers pulling in the crowd.

I've scuppered – what a relief! –
That top-heavy worm-eaten ball-breaking craft.
Though if the Earl gets wind of my drift
He'll piss himself laughing.

Let me not ruin a hard-won reputation
For mastery of bardic scholarship and skill.
I'll make sure the Earl (or former Chieftain)
Isn't in town when I give a recital.

The thing is I'm quite the draw,
Flavour of the month in certain quarters.
I'd be gone down that path like a bat from hell,
But I'm wary of the Earl –

Not to mention it was the same Hugh's son
Who once dubbed my strict verse 'easy'.
Thank God he's sojourning with the Saxon.
For the time being, I have a breather.

Those poems I pummelled into shape before
Damn near broke my heart.
This new softer more accessible approach
Will prove a tonic for my health.

And what if the Earl (the ex-Chieftain)
Quibbles now and then with a quatrain –
Aren't there plenty goms about
Who'll shout the pedant down?

The Noughties

after Immanuel Mifsud

In the electronic age every nutcase
With a notebook is writing a masterpiece;
They spend their nights locked up in chatrooms
And emerge with red eyes and love poems.

Sweet Afton

I'll sing thee a song in thy praise

Once we sparked up on planes, in lifts, playgrounds.
We smoked on the john. On the job. Even as we drove
There was a risk we took, a second of blind
Chance at the wheel to catch the light in one move.

Cigarettes broke ice when they did the rounds
At weddings, funerals. They signalled boredom
In classrooms – in the dressing room second wind,
As the team puffed at half-time and pondered the outcome.

Boys could strike a match on the seat of their pants,
While the girl in the parked car might roll one
One-handed, lick and seal the Rizla, then duck
To the flame before slowly exhaling her answer.

A priest I knew used nip out to the Gents
With a Gitane before he delivered the sermon.
You'd cadge one off the nurse, she'd wish you luck.
Hearing the news, you'd breathe deep into both lungs.

Smoke encircled the globe and perfumed the air
When we roved – it was *fumo ergo sum* on our stroll
Up rue Mouffetard to sit at dusk in the *place*
And, at the moment of love, the taste on our tongues.

O Nicotine! Sweet hay, dark plug, moist snus,
Entheogen – once balm to the workaday soul,
What became of the thrice-an-hour ritual?
That whiff of phosphor as we brought the tar

To the lips, then the draw – ah, aroma of bliss –
The one-year-in-six when we sucked the elixir?
Night, the Mardyke. I'm praying into the bowl
Of my hands, bent like a necromancer to conjure

Fire from the last match . . . it's out, blown like a kiss:
With *Woodbine, Navy Cut, Gold Leaf, Sweet Afton,*
With lino and vinyl snatched away unsung,
The fags that gave life flavour when I was young.

Postcard from San Benedetto del Tronto

The human come back to the bird colony
with plastic, fizzy drinks, scraps of fabric,
with air-filled rubber, naked offspring –
all their gull shrieks translated to Italian.

We're good at being crowds.
Some sixth sense guides us through the concourse;
we pack the terraces, or floor by floor evacuate
the tower block to gossip in the forecourt.

And here raucous outsize families spill
from Fiorinis, campervans, bulging Puntos.
They've found the beach of Hotel Hilbert
where there's always room, one more square

of burning sand to somehow fit a towel,
to plant the lounger and umbrella.
Two pedalos hired; beers; and Grandpa
with cigar is parked beside the cooler.

And though wrong-doing's infinite
(it's every man for himself in a predatory world)
the sun's decreed an amnesty,
another summer of love and ice cream.

Some voyeurism, some thievery. Keep an eye
on that Rolex: we're all sinners, but none gets knifed
or trampled, the child in difficulties will be saved,
then mobbed by a dozen flapping mamas.

Man alone is a restless pendulum:
Mr Happy, Mr Worry, Mr Mean,
popping in-and-out of quantum moods,
but, given sand and sun, the multitude

becomes a solid mass where goodness spreads
through the contagion of common needs.
Here, take my sunscreen. *Caro mio*, your ball back!
Here are my nice breasts to look at.

And here we are ourselves with scarce
six words between us, taking our bearings
from mile on mile of swingball, water pistols, Ray-Bans,
hour on hour without a thought to cloud

the blue, as we negotiate legs and lilos,
tiptoe through the simmering oiled pulchritude
to dip from time to time into the Adriatic,
swimming far out to prove its cold.

The Cranium

after Neruda

I didn't give it a thought until I was knocked down
and I heard my soul roll away in the dark.

I was dead to the world, gone – but then pain,
a spasm, and the throbbing flare of blue lights.

Later, I could pick out the moonscape of the ward,
between sleeps that felt like dirty cotton wool.

This morning my hand extended a shaky finger,
poking at the cuts and bruises, until it found

one item still whole, still game: you, poor skull –
how vainly across the years, hustling, on the prowl,

I'd examine every hair, check over each feature,
but miss the prime asset – your handsome dome

enclosing the delicate wetware of vessels
and pathways, the impossibly knotted connectors,

all that softly booming vegetal chemistry
a mini-ocean into which reason shoots bright bolts

and where, among sea-wrack and fronds of childhood,
the fish of volition darts now here, now there . . .

Where too, who knows, my timid soul hides out.
Tap-tap, knock-knock! Adam, wakey-wakey!

I'm the stonecutter on the hillside stripped clean
of trees and birdsong bowing to the trusty marble.

Or a safecracker on his knees in a vault, his ear
to the steel door, trembling for it to open.

Gone with the Wind

I couldn't remember this morning who was Scarlett O'Hara.
Olivia de Haviland, Hattie McDaniel, even Clark Gable
came to mind. I recalled Olivier. I thought of Veronica Lake.
In the end I got up and googled *Gone With the Wind*.
I have this problem with names. Celebs, exes, school friends,
with people, it seems, not places – not the 30-odd townlands
of Lisgoold: Welshtown Beg, Corracondon, Riask . . .
Later, on my run, I recalled 48 of the American states
(Wisconsin and Kentucky were the ones I missed).
But the other night I could not remember Jodie Foster,
though I chatted with her once in Leicester Square,
an ordinary college girl, between being a child star
and Agent Starling, queuing outside the Odeon
for . . . could it have been *The Company of Wolves*?
It bothered me all next day, several days, and then
on a plane held above Knock Airport, I remembered.
First I felt the shadow of a bird across a lawn, a hint
at how her name *would* sound. There was a pause
and a pressure building, but I knew I'd get there. It was
physical, like hours after lunch dislodging salami
from a tooth, first the release then the pleasure.
Then it was hard to stop. I wanted to remember them all.
Not only things buffs know, like the support role in *Once
Upon a Time in America* (that was Tuesday Weld).
But who played Dolores Haze? Who climbed the Trevi Fountain?
Who was that blonde with Cary Grant on Mount Rushmore?
Who said *Is that a gun or are you just pleased to see me?*
OK, Mae West! But why do I always first think 'Bessie Smith'?
Why does one good woman now hide behind another?
Is there some kink occurring, a hindrance in my brain?

After that I recalled the entire lineout of Cork's
1966 All-Ireland Hurling team, then went on to the rows
of boys in Junior A: Rubberneck, Horse Buckley, Squirt,
brawny gentle Brendan who died, whose nickname I will
recall – as though the brain must give the rest of life
going over what's gone before, an unforgiving effort
of retrieval: the corn field I slept in near Point du Raz,
a sand quarry outside Doneraile, girls whose faces bob
to the surface from four white winters in Ontario . . .
Let all of them be well, have prospered, each be loved.
Yet may there be the mercy of forgetting. But let me keep
to my last breath those few I'll name before I sleep tonight.

Habits

Pushing sixty, I still feed toe-clippings
to the Venus flytrap, a habit
picked up from my Aunt Kit,
then balancing on one foot
I step into track bottoms and pull on
each mismatched sock.

Downstairs, I hug the teapot to my chest
for our mutual warmth.
If I pick my nose, those pickings go
to the cactus on the sill, while
standing by the window I mouth
asshole at some unsuspecting youth.

Quits

Life's short – a blink. The wise owls tell us so.
But it's the longest span you or I will know.

Renunciation

after Séathrún Céitinn

Dear one, with your wiles,
You'd best remove your hand,
Though burning with love's fire,
I'm no more an active man.

Look at the grey on my head,
See how my body droops,
Think of my sluggish blood –
What would you have me do?

It's not desire I lack.
Don't bend low like that again.
But love without the act
May live, slender minx.

Withdraw your lips from mine,
Strong as the inclination is,
Don't brush against my skin,
That could lead to wantonness.

The intricacy of curls,
Soft eyes clear as dew,
The pale sight of your curves,
Give pleasure to me now.

Bar what the body craves,
And lying with you requires,
I'll do for our love's sake,
Dear one, with your wiles.

[36]

The Swap

for Hugo

Someone snuck over the back fence
last night and pinched my ladder.
Then I found a bronze BMX
leaning outside the front door.

Was this an ancient barter?
Oats for alcohol, salt for a new wife.
Or a neighbour's test, some version
of the Good versus the Bad Thief?

Did that man need to top leylandii?
This day take rag and bucket
to his high windows, or climb
into the dusty heat of an attic?

While I took to the roads,
blinking between the oaks
along the towpath, knowing
I was chosen for such latitude.

Faun Whistling to a Blackbird

This afternoon a blackbird came to my nook
while I was sleeping off a feed of goat curds
and retsina. I'd rented one of those dreams
from Morpheus in which I was roughing it
with A down the Glens – or was it her cousin X?
The bird startled me as she foraged near my kit,
amongst the mosses where notepad and pen
had slipped from my hand. Maybe she mistook
the pad for bread since the pages were white
with some crumbs about growing old and sex?
She took flight, but only as far as the eglantine
behind my head. I tootled to her, *Sweet bird,*
why abuse a poet lost amid his fuzzy dreams . . .
She whistled back, some Goidelic curse she'd heard
beside the Erne or Belfast Lough. Such a flyting
we had, such a duel or duet we struck up then
as our brains fired, two heated creatures reared
in muck and wind becoming soul-companions
under the Sicilian sun – her feathered, me furred.

The Nests

for Kathryn

You ask again about the nests – the wren's
hung in the ivy above the broken pier,
a goldcrest's low in the privet,
the robin's safe in the clump of pampas.
And below the Lane Gate, coal tits
have built in the hollow post.
If you run your hand up the damp shaft
you'll find the spot, where the metal is warm.
They lead us away from the house,
under the barbed wire and down the lane to the Long Field.
We'll keep in the lee of the ditch for shelter.
Overhead a mistle-thrush stirs the hawthorn,
as out in the wind the larks have settled
in cups of grass-corn for the night.
When we cross to the Glens a snipe catapults
from the rushes close by your feet.
Now we approach the wall-dark of the wood
and hear within the wounded call of an owl.
We come in due course to a river, where I lie face down
on your surface, the rain soft on my spine.

Robins

There I was turning a sod
when this bird hops along
a robin, fierce, vocal
into the path of my shovel
and nabs a glistering worm
from right under my raised arm
Why such cheek, such folly?
I hear peeps from the holly
Nestlings? No, two full-grown
birds plying their baby tune
I let fly at this fake brood
They hop higher, young hoods
and there resume the ruse
whose pitch they'll soon lose
But today the shrill refrain
says to the mother-brain
feed me so back she's driven
to my worm-of-plenty realm
and with loud bird-shouts
she orders me *out out out!*
love being such, fear errs
sundering my kingdom from hers

August

is the month of strenuous bad-omened dreams
when the sun has steadied but the heat
keeps arriving on its own momentum.
Our skins stay pale, papery, light-sensitive,
and the damp edges between us have blurred
when one afternoon ants appear from the gutters,
climbing onto flowerpots, up the thin bronze stalks.

They've sprouted wings. They're heading skywards.
It must be happening all over: this same muggy
chemical turn-on bringing about a panicky shift,
earth to air, darkness to light. The column abandons
the Roman road it's maintained all summer
from the dead hedgehog under the rhododendron
to the dust metropolis below the patio.

Out they pour for carnival, the gaudy new queens
in cellophane, the diminutive overactive males,
and take to the air swarming across south London.
When a male latches onto a queen, they'll tumble
back to earth *in flagrante* – she'll shed her wings
and burrow below ground, fertile for the winter.
I've never seen one but it works. There's no end of ants.

What we do notice are swifts, suddenly noisome,
closer to the rooftops. This is their annual ant-fest
and they've come rehearsed as shrill valkyries.
It's a beautiful sight, a swift taking an ant queen.
The bird does not slow, or swerve, but effects a pure
collision, an intersection from which the ant-speck
is gone, absorbed into the swift's arrow of flight.

Stars and Jasmine

Each of them has been a god many times:
cat, hedgehog and – our summer interloper – the tortoise.
A perfect triangle, they can neither eat
nor marry one another.
And tonight they are gods
under the jasmine under the stars.

Already the hedgehog has scoffed the cat's supper
and she's walked nonplussed beside him
escaping headlong into the bushes.
Wisely now, she keeps an eye on him there,
and on the tortoise
noisily criss-crossing the gravel.

For the cat, jasmine is white
but the stars have colours.
For the hedgehog, there are no stars
only a sky of jasmine,
against which he sniffs something dark,
outlined like a bird of prey.

Wisely, the tortoise ignores both jasmine and stars.
Isn't it enough, she says, to carry the sky on your back,
a sky that is solid, mathematical and delicately coloured –
on which someone, too, has painted
our neighbours' address: 9a Surrey Rd.
Come September, we will lower her through their letterbox.

The Water Spider

Each time the common water spider
sticks her backside up out of the garden pond
the fine hairs on her abdomen
trap air and allow her
to sink through the water with it.

There she goes, a bauble of mercury,
shimmering like a fish lure
and at risk from the carp
until she reaches the tangle of weeds,
where she's hung her silken tent.

She slides the bubble into it,
inflating a small dome – a diving bell
no engineer can match
since it exchanges dead air for oxygen
through the thin integument.

Later she builds a chamber to hatch her eggs
and lives off prey in easy reach.
Once or twice she'll come to the surface
to moult, or else fetch more air.
Later still she'll seal her capsule for the winter.

She's taken spinneret and silk to water
and skewed the theology: less fierce
than her relatives in air, she welcomes courtship
and is smaller than her male,
whom she neither eats nor poisons.

The Water Stealer

came to the pond in the night and emptied it.
I woke in the unwonted quiet
and noticed its reflections on the ceiling
absent this bright morning,

the fire outside quenched, the lilies
collapsed in a muddy heap, the neon
of damselflies, the skim of darters and fleas,
of skaters and water boatmen – gone.

Where were the carp? Sunk in the mud
or ferried into the dawn by the cormorant?
Or was it a town fox that chewed
through the tarp so it bled while I dreamt,

while my brain worried old scars,
the saucer of streetlight grew brighter
overhead and neared the huddle of carp
– who'd have jumped and bitten in terror,

gorping helplessly in the poisonous gas.

I mend the leak, and watch the basin fill,
the water not the same water: clear, drinkable,
the year's clock too far advanced to be reset,
to remake the soup of eggs and insects.

Even so, the lilies untangle and lift
their cumbersome pads off the mud –
weightless and free, like the dancers in the loft
at harvest, when I watched as a child.

But no fish . . . *the fish that came*
with the pond that came with the garden
that came with the house that came
with the care that came with the children

And the pond, which no child fell into,
recalled our old pond back in Lisgoold
and heat-struck hours with my cousins
pawdawling in the duckweed and ooze.

I'd begun, since my days are freed up,
to love its little creatures, to scoop
for springtails and 'water bear' – the minuscule
tardigrade I've seen only on YouTube.

But now a fox has come as a thief in the night
– not the fox that squeezed through the mesh
to the hencoop (which our father tracked and shot),
no, some miscreant, with a taste for fish.

It's time to cry – to pour tears like my father
in his old age, hammering the armrest
with an arthritic fist till he broke it (the armrest),
crippled because of a cur, a mongrel cur

the dog that barked that scared the mare
that carried the man that reared the foal
that loved the rider that rode the mare
that flung the rider headlong into the road

my old man, as they were galloping home
from Midleton Show, their jaunt every June
without fail till the fall . . . which would shame
and shackle him, and send him to the grave.

And now I've a fox, or worse, for adversary.
I've a night of pillage and ruin to bemoan,
robbed of my pond and its innocent creatures,
dead fish to bewail – when lo and behold

a half-dozen or so are scooting here and there
among the lilies (those long gone country dancers)
the streetwise ancient carp, yea risen out
of the mud, and me in floods at the sight.

The Face

With my grins smiles dodges
I've travelled the difficult changes
since once I was soft
with boyhood shy freckled
hid in skirts of sunlight
and looked out and up dazzled
by the laughing crowd then
sent abroad in the world flushed
with testosterone raw-boned
was caught on camera glimpsed
in wet glass or my shadow
fallen onto the still pool
how I looked back from print and screen
was scanned appraised regarded
scrutinized in sleep or
blanked across a room
in the concourse singled out
spotted in the audience
an old acquaintance
tripping on the name
for more than once I was mistaken
a country singer somebody Dutch
or Danish an upstate weatherman
how Aunt Mary believed Father
had brought pony-and-trap
that Sunday to take her
away from St Anne's
how I've been lost in thought
assumed the public guise prepared
the intimate candour given

and withheld approval been struck
down only to square up
to the day and later the dark
though I've been known to turn
aside forever slack-jawed
in stupor or daydream
how I will look on the kerb
on the slab empty of lifeblood
meanwhile I'm full of noises gifted
with muscular utterance I yield
to the yawn sneezing the giggles
am overcome by tears ecstasy surprise
I'm elastic even mesmeric
for I've travelled from life forms
that distinguished front from back
separated nutrient and toxin
nor do I omit the raptor's success
since my segments align
as instruments of attack or
defence my parts emerge
for disguise and display
so you may speak of me as
a map a blueprint remembered
in the womb a network
of switches that negotiate
between inside and out sleepless
in patrol of the edges
yet I am blank a lake where appeared
child lover father rival
and many will swear they've

observed on my bones
the ghost of a namesake
though I've come upon myself
as a canny impostor
swung around in search of some
other surely a likeness truer than this

Notes

'The Hip-Flask': up the Cydnus — Chatto & Windus.

'Irish': *Tarraingimís chuige* — let's pull towards it.

'The New Poetry': Eochaidh Ó hEoghusa, *c.*1565–1612, was Chief Poet of the O'Donnells at the time of their surrender to James II, when Hugh O'Donnell went to London to be given the title of Earl Tyrconnell.

'Sweet Afton': a brand of Irish cigarette, favoured on the Left Bank, but discontinued in 2011. The packet quoted Burns' eponymous poem: 'Flow gently, sweet Afton, amang thy green braes / Flow gently, I'll sing thee a song in thy praise.'

'Renunciation': a version of 'A bhean lán de stuaim' by Séathrún Céitinn [Geoffrey Keating], 1580–*c.*1644.